I0477894

CONTENTS

THE EMPATH EXECUTIVE'S GUIDE:
Transforming Leadership

THE EMPATH EXECUTIVE'S GUIDE:

Transforming Leadership with Compassion and Resilience

By Ammanuel Santa Anna

*with Compassion
and Resilience*

By Ammanuel Santa Anna

CHAPTER 1: UNDERSTANDING THE EMPATH EXECUTIVE

The Empath Executive: Strengths and Obstacles

As an Empath Executive, you possess a unique set of strengths that can set you apart in the business world. Your ability to understand and connect with others on a deep emotional level can be a powerful tool for building strong relationships with employees and driving innovation in the workplace. Your natural empathy allows you to see things from different perspectives, making you a more effective leader and decision-maker. However, being an empathetic executive also comes with its own set of obstacles that you must learn to navigate in order to succeed.

One of the key challenges that Empath Executives face is managing their emotions in high-pressure situations. Your heightened sensitivity to the emotions of others can make it difficult to stay calm and focused when faced with stress or conflict. Learning to regulate your own emotions and set boundaries between yourself and others is crucial for maintaining your effectiveness as a leader.

Balancing empathy with assertiveness in leadership can also be a challenge for Empath Executives. While your natural inclination may be to prioritize the needs and feelings of others, there are times when you will need to make tough decisions and assert your authority. Finding the right balance between compassion and assertiveness is essential for gaining respect and maintaining control in a leadership role.

Navigating office politics as an empathetic executive can be particularly tricky. Your ability to understand and empathize with others can make it difficult to navigate the complex dynamics of the workplace. Learning to read between the lines, set clear boundaries, and advocate for yourself and your team can help you navigate office politics with confidence and integrity.

Building strong relationships with employees as an empathetic leader is one of your greatest strengths. Your ability to connect with others on a deep emotional level can foster trust, loyalty, and collaboration within your team. By listening actively, showing empathy, and providing support, you can create a positive and productive work environment where employees feel valued and motivated to succeed.

Leveraging Empathy for Success in the Executive Role

In the fast-paced world of executive leadership, being an empath can be both a blessing and a challenge. Empath executives have a unique ability to connect with their employees on a deeper level, understand their needs, and foster a sense of trust and loyalty. However, this heightened sensitivity can also leave them vulnerable to absorbing the emotions and stresses of those around them, leading to burnout and compassion fatigue. In order to leverage empathy for success in the executive role, it is essential for empath executives to learn how to manage their emotions in high-pressure situations, balance empathy with assertiveness in leadership, and navigate office politics with grace and integrity.

One of the key strengths of empath executives is their ability to build strong relationships with their employees. By truly understanding their team members' perspectives and emotions, empath executives can create a supportive and inclusive work environment where employees feel valued and motivated to perform at their best. However, it is important for empath executives to establish clear boundaries and maintain a sense of professional distance when necessary in order to avoid becoming overwhelmed by the emotions of others.

Effective communication is another crucial skill for empath executives to master. By harnessing emotional intelligence and empathy, empath executives can communicate authentically and effectively with their team members, fostering a culture of open and honest communication. This not only helps to build trust and loyalty among employees, but also drives business success by ensuring that everyone is on the same page and working towards a common goal.

In addition to communication, empath executives can also leverage their empathy to drive innovation and creativity in the workplace. By encouraging diversity of thought and valuing different perspectives, empath executives can inspire their team members to think outside the box, take risks, and come up with innovative solutions to complex problems. This not only fosters a culture of creativity and innovation, but also sets the stage for long-term success and growth for the organization.

Ultimately, being an empath executive is a delicate balancing act. By leveraging their unique strengths, managing their emotions, and communicating effectively, empath executives can lead with authenticity and vulnerability, empower and inspire their employees, and drive business success in a way that is both compassionate and effective. With the right mindset and skills, empath executives can overcome the obstacles they may face and thrive in the executive role, making a positive impact on their team, their organization, and the world around them.

CHAPTER 2: MANAGING EMOTIONS IN HIGH-PRESSURE SITUATIONS

Recognizing Triggers and Managing Emotional Responses

As an Empath Executive, it is crucial to recognize the triggers that can lead to emotional responses in high-pressure situations. Whether it be a demanding project deadline or a difficult conversation with a team member, understanding what sets off your emotions is the first step in effectively managing them. By identifying these triggers, you can develop strategies to navigate them and maintain a sense of calm and control in the face of adversity.

Managing emotions in the workplace can be especially challenging for Empath Executives, as they are more attuned to the feelings of those around them. It is important to find a balance between empathy and assertiveness in leadership, ensuring that you are able to connect with your team members on a personal level while still making tough decisions when necessary. By setting boundaries and communicating clearly, Empath Executives can effectively navigate office politics and maintain their emotional well-being in the workplace.

Building strong relationships with employees is a key aspect of empathetic leadership. By showing empathy and understanding towards your team members, you can create a supportive and inclusive work environment where everyone feels valued and respected. This can lead to increased employee satisfaction, motivation, and productivity, ultimately driving business success.

One of the biggest challenges for Empath Executives is overcoming burnout and compassion fatigue. The demands of the executive role can be overwhelming, and it is important to prioritize self-care and set boundaries to prevent emotional exhaustion. By practicing mindfulness, seeking support from colleagues or a professional coach, and taking regular breaks to recharge, Empath Executives can avoid burnout and continue to lead with authenticity and vulnerability.

In conclusion, recognizing triggers and managing emotional responses is essential for Empath Executives to succeed in their roles. By balancing empathy with assertiveness, navigating office politics with grace, building strong relationships with employees, and prioritizing self-care, Empath Executives can harness their unique strengths to drive innovation, creativity, and business success in the workplace. By leading with authenticity and vulnerability, Empath Executives can empower and inspire their teams to reach their full potential.

Strategies for Staying Calm and Focused Under Pressure

In the fast-paced world of business, executives are often faced with high-pressure situations that require them to stay calm and focused in order to make sound decisions. For Empath Executives, who are highly attuned to the emotions of others, this can be particularly challenging. However, there are strategies that can help Empath Executives navigate these stressful moments with grace and composure.

One key strategy for staying calm and focused under pressure is to practice mindfulness and meditation. By taking a few moments each day to center yourself and quiet your mind, you can build resilience and create a sense of inner calm that will serve you well in high-pressure situations. Additionally, mindfulness can help Empath Executives stay present and focused on the task at hand, rather than getting lost in the emotions of those around them.

Another important strategy for Empath Executives is to set boundaries and prioritize self-care. It can be easy for Empath Executives to become overwhelmed by the emotions of others, leading to burnout and compassion fatigue. By setting clear boundaries and taking time to recharge and care for yourself, you can better manage your own emotions and stay focused and centered in high-pressure situations.

Balancing empathy with assertiveness is another crucial skill for Empath Executives to master. While empathy is a valuable asset in building strong relationships with employees and driving innovation in the workplace, it is also important for Empath Executives to assert themselves and set clear expectations. By finding the right balance between empathy and assertiveness, Empath Executives can effectively lead their teams while staying true to their empathetic nature.

In addition to these strategies, Empath Executives can benefit from developing their emotional intelligence and communication skills. By honing their ability to read and understand the emotions of others, Empath Executives can better navigate office politics and build strong relationships with their employees. Effective communication is also key for Empath Executives, as it allows them to convey their ideas and vision clearly and inspire and empower their teams.

Overall, by leveraging their unique strengths as Empath Executives and implementing these strategies for staying calm and focused under pressure, leaders can drive business success, foster innovation, and create a positive and supportive work environment for their employees. By embracing their empathy and using it as a tool for effective leadership, Empath Executives can truly make a difference in the world of business.

CHAPTER 3: BALANCING EMPATHY WITH ASSERTIVENESS IN LEADERSHIP

Setting Boundaries as an Empathetic Leader

Setting boundaries as an empathetic leader is crucial in maintaining balance and harmony in the workplace. Empath executives have a natural tendency to absorb the emotions and energy of those around them, which can lead to feeling overwhelmed and drained. By setting clear boundaries, empathetic leaders can protect their own well-being while still being supportive and compassionate towards their team members.

One important boundary to establish as an empathetic leader is the distinction between empathy and enabling. While it is important to show understanding and support to employees, it is also necessary to hold them accountable for their actions and behaviors. Setting boundaries around what is acceptable in the workplace and enforcing consequences for inappropriate behavior can help maintain a healthy and productive work environment.

Balancing empathy with assertiveness is another key aspect of setting boundaries as an empathetic leader. It is important to be able to empathize with employees and understand their perspectives, while also being able to make tough decisions and hold firm to expectations. By finding the right balance between empathy and assertiveness, empathetic leaders can effectively lead their teams while still maintaining a compassionate and understanding approach.

Navigating office politics as an empathetic executive can be particularly challenging, as empathetic leaders may struggle with confrontation and conflict. Setting boundaries around how to handle office politics, such as maintaining neutrality and focusing on solutions rather than getting caught up in drama, can help empathetic leaders navigate these complex situations with grace and professionalism.

Building strong relationships with employees as an empathetic leader is essential for creating a positive and supportive work environment. By setting boundaries around communication, feedback, and expectations, empathetic leaders can foster trust and respect among their team members. This can lead to increased employee engagement, satisfaction, and productivity, ultimately driving business success.

Assertive Communication Techniques for Empath Executives

Assertive communication is a crucial skill for empath executives to master in order to navigate the complexities of leadership while staying true to their empathetic nature. By blending empathy with assertiveness, empath executives can effectively communicate their needs, boundaries, and expectations in a way that is both respectful and impactful. One key technique for assertive communication is using "I" statements to express thoughts and feelings without blaming or accusing others. For example, instead of saying "You never listen to me," an empath executive could say, "I feel unheard when my ideas are not taken into consideration."

In high-pressure situations, managing emotions is essential

for empath executives to maintain their composure and make rational decisions. By practicing mindfulness techniques such as deep breathing, meditation, or visualization, empath executives can regulate their emotions and stay focused on the task at hand. Additionally, setting boundaries and taking breaks when needed can help prevent burnout and compassion fatigue, allowing empath executives to recharge and approach challenges with a clear mind.

Balancing empathy with assertiveness in leadership requires empath executives to find a middle ground between being too passive or too aggressive. By listening actively to their employees, showing understanding and compassion, and offering support, empath executives can build strong relationships based on trust and mutual respect. When it comes to making tough decisions or addressing conflicts, assertive communication techniques can help empath executives assert their authority while still showing empathy and understanding towards others.

In navigating office politics, empathetic executives can leverage their emotional intelligence to read between the lines, understand different perspectives, and build alliances based on trust and integrity. By staying authentic and true to their values, empath executives can lead by example and inspire their team to do the same. Building strong relationships with employees through empathy and vulnerability can create a positive and inclusive work environment where everyone feels valued and supported.

In conclusion, empath executives have a unique set of strengths and challenges that can be leveraged for success in the business world. By mastering assertive communication techniques, managing emotions effectively, balancing empathy with assertiveness, navigating office politics with integrity, and building strong relationships with employees, empath executives can drive innovation, inspire their team, and lead with authenticity and vulnerability. By harnessing the power of empathy and emotional intelligence, empath executives can create a workplace culture that fosters creativity, collaboration, and growth.

CHAPTER 4: NAVIGATING OFFICE POLITICS AS AN EMPATHETIC EXECUTIVE

Building Alliances and Handling Conflict Diplomatically

Building alliances and handling conflict diplomatically are essential skills for Empath Executives to master in order to navigate the complex world of leadership. As an empathetic leader, it is important to build strong relationships with employees and colleagues in order to foster a positive and productive work environment. By taking the time to understand the needs and motivations of others, Empath Executives can create alliances that are based on trust and mutual respect.

When conflict arises in the workplace, it is crucial for Empath Executives to approach the situation with empathy and understanding. By actively listening to all parties involved and seeking to find common ground, conflicts can often be resolved in a way that is beneficial for everyone. It is important for Empath Executives to remain calm and composed in high-pressure situations, using their emotional intelligence to guide their actions and responses.

Balancing empathy with assertiveness in leadership is another key aspect of being an Empath Executive. While it is important to be empathetic and understanding towards others, it is also essential to set boundaries and hold employees accountable for their actions. By finding a balance between empathy and assertiveness, Empath Executives can effectively lead their teams towards success while maintaining a positive and supportive work environment.

Navigating office politics as an empathetic executive can be challenging, but by remaining true to their values and principles, Empath Executives can avoid getting caught up in power struggles and conflicts. By focusing on building strong relationships with colleagues and employees, Empath Executives can create a network of support that will help them navigate office politics with grace and integrity.

In order to avoid burnout and compassion fatigue, Empath Executives must prioritize self-care and set boundaries to protect their emotional well-being. By practicing mindfulness, seeking support from colleagues and mentors, and taking time to recharge, Empath Executives can avoid burnout and continue to lead with authenticity and vulnerability. By harnessing their empathy to drive innovation and creativity in the workplace, Empath Executives can inspire and empower their teams to achieve greatness.

Strategies for Maintaining Integrity in a Competitive Environment

In today's competitive business environment, it can be challenging for empath executives to maintain their integrity while navigating the pressures of leadership. However, there are strategies that empath executives can employ to stay true to their values and lead with authenticity. One key strategy is to prioritize self-care and emotional well-being. Empath executives often absorb the emotions of those around them, which can lead to burnout and compassion fatigue. By taking time for self-care, whether through mindfulness practices, exercise, or hobbies that bring joy, empath executives can recharge and better manage their emotions in high-pressure situations.

Another important strategy for maintaining integrity in a competitive environment is to balance empathy with assertiveness in leadership. Empaths have a natural ability to understand and connect with others, but they may struggle with being assertive or making tough decisions that could impact their team or organization. By finding a balance between empathy and assertiveness, empath executives can effectively lead their teams while staying true to their values. This may involve setting clear boundaries, communicating expectations clearly, and making decisions that align with the organization's mission and goals.

Navigating office politics can be another obstacle for empath executives, as they may struggle with the cutthroat nature of competition. To maintain integrity in this environment, empath executives can focus on building strong relationships with their employees. By creating a culture of trust, transparency, and open communication, empath executives can foster a sense of unity and collaboration within their teams. This not only helps to mitigate office politics but also creates a supportive and positive work environment where employees feel valued and respected.

Using emotional intelligence to drive business success is another key strategy for empath executives looking to maintain integrity in a competitive environment. Empaths have a heightened sense of emotional awareness, which can be a powerful tool for building strong relationships with clients, employees, and stakeholders. By harnessing their emotional intelligence, empath executives can effectively communicate, inspire, and motivate others, driving innovation and creativity in the workplace. This can lead to increased productivity, employee engagement, and overall business success.

In conclusion, maintaining integrity as an empath executive in a competitive environment requires a combination of self-care, emotional intelligence, assertiveness, and relationship-building skills. By prioritizing these strategies, empath executives can lead with authenticity and vulnerability, empower their employees, and drive business success. By leveraging their unique strengths and overcoming obstacles, empath executives can thrive in their roles and make a positive impact on their organizations.

CHAPTER 5: BUILDING STRONG RELATIONSHIPS WITH EMPLOYEES AS AN EMPATHETIC LEADER

Empathy in Employee Relations: Building Trust and Loyalty

As an Empath Executive, one of your greatest strengths is your ability to understand and connect with the emotions of others. This unique skill set can be a powerful tool in building trust and loyalty among your employees. By demonstrating empathy in your interactions with your team members, you can create a sense of psychological safety that encourages open communication and collaboration. This, in turn, can lead to higher levels of engagement and productivity within your organization.

Managing emotions in high-pressure situations is a key aspect of being an Empath Executive. By harnessing your empathy, you can navigate stressful situations with grace and composure, inspiring confidence in your leadership abilities. By staying calm and collected in the face of adversity, you can set an example for your employees and help them feel supported and valued.

Balancing empathy with assertiveness in leadership is another important skill for Empath Executives to master. While it is crucial to understand and validate the emotions of others, it is also important to set clear boundaries and hold people accountable for their actions. By finding the right balance between empathy and assertiveness, you can create a culture of accountability and respect within your organization.

Navigating office politics as an empathetic executive can be challenging, as you may be more sensitive to the emotions and motivations of others. However, by staying true to your values and maintaining open lines of communication, you can navigate tricky political situations with integrity and grace. By approaching office politics with empathy and authenticity, you can build strong relationships with your colleagues and earn their trust and loyalty.

Building strong relationships with employees as an empathetic leader is essential for driving success in your organization. By showing genuine care and concern for your team members, you can create a positive work environment where people feel valued and supported. By listening to their concerns, providing feedback, and offering guidance, you can foster a sense of loyalty and commitment among your employees that will drive long-term success for your organization.

Creating a Positive and Supportive Work Environment

Creating a positive and supportive work environment is essential for Empath Executives to thrive in their roles. As leaders who are highly attuned to the emotions of others, it is important to set the tone for a workplace that values empathy, compassion, and collaboration. By fostering a culture of support and understanding, Empath Executives can create a space where employees feel valued, heard, and appreciated.

Managing emotions in high-pressure situations is a crucial skill for Empath Executives. In times of stress or conflict, it can be easy to become overwhelmed by the emotions of others. By practicing mindfulness and self-care techniques, Empath Executives can maintain their emotional balance and make sound decisions in challenging situations. Setting boundaries and taking time for self-reflection can also help Empath Executives navigate high-pressure environments with grace and resilience.

Balancing empathy with assertiveness in leadership is a delicate dance for Empath Executives. While empathy is a valuable trait that allows leaders to connect with their teams on a deeper level, it is also important to assert boundaries and make tough decisions when necessary. By finding the right balance between empathy and assertiveness, Empath Executives can lead with confidence and compassion, inspiring their teams to perform at their best.

Navigating office politics as an empathetic executive can be challenging, as Empath Executives may struggle with the cutthroat nature of corporate environments. By staying true to their values and principles, Empath Executives can build strong relationships with colleagues and navigate office politics with integrity and grace. By cultivating a network of supportive allies and mentors, Empath Executives can overcome obstacles and achieve success in their careers.

Building strong relationships with employees as an empathetic leader is key to creating a positive and productive work environment. By listening actively, showing empathy, and providing support, Empath Executives can foster trust and loyalty among their teams. By recognizing and celebrating the unique strengths and contributions of each team member, Empath Executives can empower their employees to reach their full potential and drive business success.

CHAPTER 6: OVERCOMING BURNOUT AND COMPASSION FATIGUE IN THE EXECUTIVE ROLE

Recognizing the Signs of Burnout and Compassion Fatigue

Recognizing the signs of burnout and compassion fatigue is crucial for Empath Executives who often find themselves in high-pressure situations. As leaders who prioritize empathy and understanding, it can be easy to neglect self-care and become overwhelmed by the demands of the role. Burnout and compassion fatigue can manifest in various ways, such as feeling emotionally drained, experiencing physical symptoms like fatigue and headaches, or becoming irritable and detached from others. By recognizing these signs early on, Empath Executives can take proactive steps to prevent further deterioration of their mental and emotional well-being.

It is essential for Empath Executives to balance their empathy with assertiveness in leadership to avoid burnout and compassion fatigue. While it is important to connect with employees on a personal level and show understanding towards their emotions, it is equally crucial to set boundaries and assert oneself when needed. By finding the right balance between empathy and assertiveness, Empath Executives can effectively lead their teams without sacrificing their own well-being. This balance allows them to navigate office politics with integrity and authenticity, building strong relationships with employees based on trust and mutual respect.

Building strong relationships with employees as an empathetic leader is key to fostering a positive work environment and driving business success. Empath Executives have a unique ability to connect with their team members on a deeper level, understanding their needs and motivations. By leveraging their emotional intelligence and communication skills, Empath Executives can empower and inspire employees to perform at their best. This not only boosts morale and productivity but also creates a culture of collaboration and innovation within the workplace.

To overcome burnout and compassion fatigue, Empath Executives must prioritize self-care and emotional well-being. This may involve setting boundaries, practicing mindfulness and stress management techniques, seeking support from mentors or therapists, and taking regular breaks to recharge. By recognizing the signs of burnout and compassion fatigue early on and implementing healthy coping strategies, Empath Executives can continue to lead with authenticity and vulnerability, harnessing empathy to drive innovation and creativity in the workplace. Ultimately, by taking care of themselves, Empath Executives can better serve their teams and achieve long-term success in their roles.

Self-Care Strategies for Empathetic Executives

As an empathetic executive, it is crucial to prioritize self-care in order to effectively lead and manage others. The unique strengths and obstacles that come with being both an executive and an empath can be draining, so it is important to have a robust self-care routine in place. One key strategy for self-care is setting boundaries. Empaths often have trouble saying no and can become overwhelmed by taking on too much. By setting clear boundaries and learning to say no when necessary, empathetic executives can prevent burnout and maintain their well-being.

Another important self-care strategy for empathetic executives is practicing mindfulness and meditation. These techniques can help executives manage their emotions in high-pressure situations, stay present in the moment, and cultivate a sense of inner peace. By incorporating mindfulness into their daily routine, empathetic executives can better navigate the stress and challenges that come with their role.

Balancing empathy with assertiveness in leadership is another key aspect of self-care for empathetic executives. It is important to be compassionate and understanding towards employees, while also being able to make tough decisions and hold others accountable. Finding this balance can be challenging, but it is essential for effective leadership. Empathetic executives can benefit from practicing assertiveness techniques and seeking out mentorship or coaching to help them navigate this balance.

Navigating office politics as an empathetic executive can be particularly challenging, as empaths may struggle with confrontation and conflict. Self-care in this context involves developing strategies for handling difficult conversations, setting clear expectations with colleagues, and seeking support from trusted allies within the organization. By prioritizing their own well-being and emotional health, empathetic executives can navigate office politics more effectively and build strong relationships with their colleagues.

In conclusion, self-care is essential for empathetic executives to thrive in their roles and lead with authenticity and vulnerability. By prioritizing boundaries, mindfulness, assertiveness, and navigating office politics with care, empathetic executives can overcome burnout and compassion fatigue, drive business success through emotional intelligence, and inspire and empower their employees. By harnessing their empathy and leveraging their unique strengths, empathetic executives can create a positive and innovative workplace culture that benefits both themselves and their teams.

CHAPTER 7: USING EMOTIONAL INTELLIGENCE TO DRIVE BUSINESS SUCCESS

Leveraging Emotional Intelligence for Effective Decision-Making

In the world of business, decision-making is a critical component of success. As an Empath Executive, it is important to leverage your emotional intelligence to make effective decisions that not only benefit the bottom line but also take into consideration the well-being of your employees and the overall company culture. By tapping into your empathetic nature, you can better understand the needs and emotions of those around you, leading to more thoughtful and compassionate decision-making.

Managing emotions in high-pressure situations is a common challenge for many executives, but as an empath, you have a unique advantage. By harnessing your emotional intelligence, you can remain calm and composed in stressful situations, allowing you to make clear and rational decisions. This ability to stay level-headed under pressure can set you apart as a leader who inspires trust and confidence among your team.

Balancing empathy with assertiveness in leadership is another key skill for Empath Executives to master. While empathy is a valuable trait that allows you to connect with others on a deeper level, it is important to also assert your authority when necessary. By finding the right balance between empathy and assertiveness, you can lead with compassion while still driving results and maintaining boundaries within the organization.

Navigating office politics as an empathetic executive can be challenging, as you may be more sensitive to the emotions and dynamics at play in the workplace. However, by using your emotional intelligence to read the room and understand the motivations of others, you can navigate office politics with grace and diplomacy. By approaching these situations with empathy and integrity, you can build trust and goodwill among your colleagues.

Building strong relationships with employees as an empathetic leader is essential for creating a positive and productive work environment. By demonstrating empathy and understanding towards your team members, you can foster loyalty and trust, leading to higher levels of engagement and performance. By leveraging your emotional intelligence to connect with your employees on a personal level, you can build a strong foundation of trust and mutual respect that will benefit both the individuals and the organization as a whole.

Emotional Intelligence in Negotiations and Conflict Resolution

Emotional intelligence plays a crucial role in negotiations and conflict resolution for Empath Executives. As leaders who are highly attuned to the emotions of others, it is essential to leverage this strength in high-pressure situations. By understanding and managing their own emotions effectively, Empath Executives can navigate challenging negotiations with grace and composure. This ability to stay calm under pressure can help them make rational decisions and find mutually beneficial solutions in conflict resolution scenarios.

Balancing empathy with assertiveness is another key aspect of emotional intelligence for Empath Executives in leadership roles. While it is important to show compassion and understanding towards others, it is equally important to assert boundaries and communicate assertively when needed. By finding the right balance between empathy and assertiveness, Empath Executives can lead their teams effectively and resolve conflicts with confidence and clarity.

Navigating office politics as an empathetic executive can be a challenging task. Empath Executives may find themselves caught in the middle of conflicts or power struggles within the organization. By harnessing their emotional intelligence, they can navigate these tricky situations with tact and diplomacy. Building strong relationships with employees is key to successful leadership as an Empath Executive. By showing genuine care and empathy towards their team members, Empath Executives can inspire loyalty, trust, and collaboration within their organization.

Overcoming burnout and compassion fatigue is a common challenge for Empath Executives in demanding leadership roles. By prioritizing self-care and setting boundaries, they can prevent burnout and maintain their emotional well-being. Using emotional intelligence to drive business success is a powerful tool for Empath Executives. By understanding the emotions and motivations of their team members and stakeholders, they can make strategic decisions that drive innovation and creativity in the workplace. Overall, by leading with authenticity, vulnerability, and empathy, Empath Executives can empower and inspire their employees to reach their full potential and achieve success as a team.

CHAPTER 8: COMMUNICATING EFFECTIVELY AS AN EMPATHETIC LEADER

Active Listening and Empathetic Communication Skills

Active listening and empathetic communication skills are essential tools for Empath Executives to succeed in their roles. These skills allow executives to connect with their employees on a deeper level, understand their needs and concerns, and build strong relationships based on trust and empathy.

One of the key aspects of active listening is the ability to fully engage with the speaker, showing genuine interest in their thoughts and feelings. Empath Executives can use their natural empathy to not only listen to what is being said but also to tune into the emotions behind the words. This level of attentiveness helps to foster a sense of understanding and validation, making employees feel heard and valued.

Empathetic communication goes beyond just listening – it involves responding in a way that shows empathy and understanding. This means acknowledging and validating the emotions of others, even if you may not agree with their perspective. Empath Executives can use their emotional intelligence to navigate difficult conversations with grace and compassion, ultimately strengthening their relationships with their team members.

Balancing empathy with assertiveness in leadership is a common challenge for Empath Executives. While it is important to be empathetic and understanding, it is also crucial to set boundaries, make tough decisions, and hold employees accountable. By mastering the art of assertive communication, empathetic leaders can maintain a healthy balance between compassion and authority, earning respect and trust from their team.

Overall, developing active listening and empathetic communication skills is essential for Empath Executives to thrive in their roles. By leveraging their natural strengths of empathy and emotional intelligence, these leaders can create a positive and supportive work environment, drive innovation and creativity, and inspire their employees to reach their full potential.

Giving and Receiving Constructive Feedback with Empathy

Giving and receiving constructive feedback is a crucial aspect of leadership, especially for Empath Executives who value empathy and understanding in their interactions with others. When it comes to providing feedback, it is important to approach the conversation with empathy and compassion. Remember that feedback is not about pointing out flaws or mistakes, but rather about helping others grow and improve. By delivering feedback in a constructive and empathetic manner, you can build trust and rapport with your employees, fostering a positive and supportive work environment.

As an Empath Executive, it is equally important to be open to receiving feedback from others. While it can be challenging to hear criticism, especially for those who are highly empathetic, it is essential to see feedback as an opportunity for growth and self-improvement. Approach feedback with an open mind and a willingness to learn from others' perspectives. By demonstrating vulnerability and a willingness to listen, you can create a culture of openness and trust within your organization.

Balancing empathy with assertiveness in leadership is a delicate dance that Empath Executives must master. While empathy is a valuable trait that can help you connect with others on a deeper level, assertiveness is necessary for making tough decisions and driving results. Finding the right balance between empathy and assertiveness can be challenging, but it is essential for effective leadership. Remember that being empathetic does not mean being a pushover – it means understanding and considering the feelings of others while still maintaining your leadership role.

Navigating office politics as an empathetic executive can also present unique challenges. Empaths may find themselves caught in the middle of conflicts or struggling to assert themselves in competitive environments. To navigate office politics successfully, Empath Executives must rely on their emotional intelligence and ability to read social cues. By remaining authentic and true to their values, empathetic leaders can build strong relationships and navigate office politics with integrity.

In conclusion, giving and receiving constructive feedback with empathy is a key skill for Empath Executives to develop. By approaching feedback conversations with compassion and understanding, empathetic leaders can foster a positive and supportive work environment. Balancing empathy with assertiveness, navigating office politics, and building strong relationships with employees are all essential aspects of leadership for Empath Executives. By leveraging their unique strengths and abilities, Empath Executives can drive business success, inspire their teams, and create a workplace culture that values empathy and authenticity.

CHAPTER 9: HARNESSING EMPATHY TO DRIVE INNOVATION AND CREATIVITY IN THE WORKPLACE

Fostering a Culture of Psychological Safety and Creativity

Fostering a culture of psychological safety and creativity is essential for Empath Executives to thrive in their roles. As leaders who value empathy and understanding, creating a safe space for employees to express themselves without fear of judgment is crucial. When employees feel psychologically safe, they are more likely to take risks, share innovative ideas, and collaborate effectively with their peers. This environment of openness and trust can lead to increased creativity and productivity within the organization.

Managing emotions in high-pressure situations is a common challenge for Empath Executives. The ability to regulate one's emotions and remain calm under pressure is key to making sound decisions and leading effectively. By practicing mindfulness techniques, such as deep breathing or visualization, Empath

Executives can stay grounded and focused during stressful situations. Additionally, seeking support from a mentor, coach, or therapist can help them navigate their emotions and develop healthy coping mechanisms.

Balancing empathy with assertiveness in leadership is a delicate dance for Empath Executives. While it is important to show compassion and understanding towards employees, it is also crucial to set clear boundaries and hold individuals accountable for their actions. By communicating expectations clearly and providing constructive feedback, Empath Executives can strike a balance between being empathetic and assertive in their leadership style. This approach can help foster a culture of accountability and high performance within the organization.

Navigating office politics as an empathetic executive can be challenging, as Empath Executives may be more sensitive to power dynamics and interpersonal relationships. By staying true to their values and maintaining open communication with colleagues, Empath Executives can navigate office politics with integrity and authenticity. Building strong relationships with employees as an empathetic leader is key to earning trust and loyalty from team members. By actively listening, showing empathy, and providing support, Empath Executives can create a positive work environment where employees feel valued and appreciated.

In conclusion, Empath Executives can leverage their unique strengths to foster a culture of psychological safety and creativity within their organizations. By managing emotions effectively, balancing empathy with assertiveness, navigating office politics with integrity, and building strong relationships with employees, Empath Executives can lead with authenticity and drive innovation in the workplace. By harnessing empathy to inspire and empower employees, Empath Executives can create a positive and nurturing work environment that promotes creativity, collaboration, and success.

Encouraging Diverse Perspectives and Empathetic Collaboration

Encouraging diverse perspectives and empathetic collaboration is essential for Empath Executives in order to harness the full potential of their unique strengths. By actively seeking out and valuing different viewpoints, Empath Executives can create a more inclusive and innovative work environment where all voices are heard and respected. This not only enhances team dynamics, but also leads to more creative solutions to complex problems.

One key aspect of encouraging diverse perspectives is fostering a culture of empathy within the organization. Empath Executives should lead by example, demonstrating understanding and compassion towards their colleagues and employees. By showing empathy in their interactions, Empath Executives can create a safe space for others to express their thoughts and opinions without fear of judgment or criticism.

Empath Executives must also strike a balance between empathy and assertiveness in their leadership style. While empathy is a valuable trait that allows them to connect with others on a deeper level, they must also be able to make tough decisions and set clear boundaries when necessary. By finding the right balance between empathy and assertiveness, Empath Executives can effectively lead their teams while still maintaining a sense of compassion and understanding.

Navigating office politics can be particularly challenging for Empath Executives, as they may be more sensitive to interpersonal conflicts and power dynamics. To overcome these obstacles, Empath Executives should focus on building strong relationships with their colleagues and employees based on trust, honesty, and open communication. By cultivating a supportive and collaborative work environment, Empath Executives can navigate office politics more effectively and build a strong foundation for success.

In conclusion, encouraging diverse perspectives and empathetic collaboration is vital for Empath Executives to leverage their strengths for success. By valuing empathy, fostering a culture of understanding, and striking a balance between compassion and assertiveness, Empath Executives can lead with authenticity and vulnerability, inspire their teams, and drive innovation and creativity in the workplace. By using emotional intelligence to drive business success, communicating effectively, and empowering employees through empathetic leadership, Empath Executives can overcome burnout and compassion fatigue, and create a work environment where everyone feels valued and supported.

CHAPTER 10: LEADING WITH AUTHENTICITY AND VULNERABILITY AS AN EXECUTIVE EMPATH

Embracing Vulnerability as a Strength in Leadership

In the fast-paced world of business, vulnerability is often seen as a weakness. However, for empath executives, embracing vulnerability can actually be a strength in leadership. By being open and honest about their emotions and struggles, empath executives can build stronger connections with their team members and inspire trust and loyalty.

One of the key strengths of empath executives is their ability to manage emotions in high-pressure situations. By acknowledging their vulnerability and seeking support when needed, empath executives can navigate stressful circumstances with grace and resilience. This emotional intelligence allows them to make more thoughtful and strategic decisions, even in the face of adversity.

Balancing empathy with assertiveness is another challenge that empath executives face. It is important for them to find a way to be compassionate and understanding while also setting clear boundaries and expectations. By learning to assert themselves in a kind and respectful manner, empath executives can effectively lead their team members and drive positive results.

Navigating office politics can be especially challenging for empathetic leaders. It is important for them to stay true to their values and principles while also building strong relationships with key stakeholders. By approaching office politics with empathy and authenticity, empath executives can foster a positive and inclusive work environment for their team members.

Overall, embracing vulnerability as a strength in leadership is essential for empath executives. By being authentic and transparent about their emotions and experiences, empath executives can empower and inspire their team members to reach their full potential. In doing so, they can drive innovation, creativity, and success in the workplace while also fostering a culture of empathy and understanding.

Cultivating Authentic Leadership Presence and Connection

As an Empath Executive, it is essential to cultivate an authentic leadership presence and connection with those around you. Your unique ability to understand and relate to the emotions of others can be a powerful tool in building strong relationships with your employees and driving business success. However, it is important to find a balance between empathy and assertiveness in your leadership style. By harnessing your emotional intelligence and using it to communicate effectively, you can inspire and empower those around you.

Managing emotions in high-pressure situations is a common challenge for Empath Executives. It can be easy to become overwhelmed by the emotions of others or to take on too much responsibility for their well-being. To avoid burnout and compassion fatigue, it is important to set boundaries and prioritize self-care. By taking care of yourself, you can better support and lead your team.

Navigating office politics as an empathetic executive can be tricky. It is important to stay true to your values and maintain your authenticity, even in challenging situations. By building strong relationships with your colleagues based on trust and empathy, you can navigate office politics with integrity and grace. Remember to stay true to yourself and your values, even when faced with difficult decisions.

Building strong relationships with your employees as an empathetic leader is essential for creating a positive and productive work environment. By listening to their needs and concerns, showing empathy and understanding, and providing support and guidance, you can inspire and empower your team to succeed. Remember to lead with authenticity and vulnerability, and to always communicate openly and honestly with your employees.

In conclusion, being an Empath Executive comes with its own set of unique strengths and obstacles. By leveraging your strengths, managing your emotions, balancing empathy with assertiveness, navigating office politics, building strong relationships, and leading with authenticity and vulnerability, you can drive innovation, inspire your team, and achieve success in your executive role. Remember to prioritize self-care, communicate effectively, and harness your empathy to create a positive and productive work environment for yourself and those around you.

CHAPTER 11: EMPOWERING AND INSPIRING EMPLOYEES THROUGH EMPATHETIC LEADERSHIP

Motivating and Engaging Employees with Empathy

As an Empath Executive, one of your greatest strengths lies in your ability to connect with and understand the emotions of those around you. This unique trait can be a powerful tool for motivating and engaging your employees in the workplace. By showing empathy towards their concerns, struggles, and successes, you can create a more positive and supportive work environment where everyone feels valued and appreciated.

Managing emotions in high-pressure situations is another key skill that Empath Executives excel in. When faced with challenging circumstances or difficult decisions, it is important to remain calm and composed while still acknowledging the emotions of those involved. By staying grounded and focused on finding solutions, you can inspire confidence and trust in your leadership abilities.

Balancing empathy with assertiveness in leadership is a delicate dance that Empath Executives must master. While it is important to be compassionate and understanding towards your employees, it is equally important to set clear expectations and hold them accountable for their performance. By finding the right balance between empathy and assertiveness, you can effectively lead your team towards success while still fostering a supportive and nurturing work culture.

Navigating office politics as an empathetic executive can be a challenging task. It is important to remain neutral and unbiased in your interactions with colleagues, while still showing empathy towards their concerns and perspectives. By staying true to your values and principles, you can build trust and credibility among your peers while still maintaining a sense of authenticity and integrity in your leadership role.

Building strong relationships with employees as an empathetic leader is essential for creating a positive and productive work environment. By taking the time to listen to their needs, concerns, and feedback, you can foster a sense of trust and loyalty among your team members. This, in turn, can lead to increased engagement, motivation, and job satisfaction, ultimately driving business success and growth.

Empowering Employees to Reach Their Full Potential with Compassionate Leadership

Empath Executives have a unique set of strengths and obstacles that come with their ability to deeply understand and connect with others on an emotional level. One of the key challenges faced by Empath Executives is finding the balance between empathy and assertiveness in their leadership style. While empathy is a valuable trait that can help build strong relationships with employees and drive innovation in the workplace, it can also be perceived as a weakness if not balanced with assertiveness. Compassionate leadership is about empowering employees to reach their full potential by creating a supportive and nurturing environment where they feel valued and understood.

Managing emotions in high-pressure situations is a crucial skill for Empath Executives, as they are often more sensitive to the emotions of others and may absorb the stress and anxiety of their team members. By practicing self-awareness and self-regulation, Empath Executives can maintain their composure and make clear, rational decisions even in the most challenging circumstances. It is important for Empath Executives to prioritize self-care and set boundaries to prevent burnout and compassion fatigue, which can be common pitfalls for those in leadership roles who are constantly giving their energy and empathy to others.

Navigating office politics as an empathetic executive can be a delicate balancing act, as Empath Executives may find themselves caught in the middle of conflicts and power struggles due to their ability to see multiple perspectives. By staying true to their values and principles, Empath Executives can build trust and credibility with their team members and colleagues, fostering a positive and inclusive work culture. Building strong relationships with employees as an empathetic leader is essential for creating a cohesive and high-performing team. By actively listening, showing empathy, and providing support and guidance, Empath Executives can inspire and empower their employees to excel in their roles and contribute to the overall success of the organization.

Using emotional intelligence to drive business success is a key strength of Empath Executives, as they are able to understand and connect with others on a deeper level, leading to more effective communication, collaboration, and decision-making. By harnessing empathy to drive innovation and creativity in the workplace, Empath Executives can inspire their team members to think outside the box and bring fresh perspectives to problem-solving. Leading with authenticity and vulnerability as an executive empath is about being true to oneself and transparent with others, creating an atmosphere of trust and openness that encourages creativity, collaboration, and growth. Empowering and inspiring employees through empathetic leadership is a powerful way for Empath Executives to leverage their strengths and create a positive impact on their team and organization. By fostering a culture of empathy, compassion, and support, Empath Executives can create a workplace where employees feel valued, motivated, and empowered to reach their full potential.

CONCLUSION: EMBRACING YOUR EMPATHETIC LEADERSHIP JOURNEY

In conclusion, embracing your empathetic leadership journey is not just about being a compassionate leader, but also about leveraging your unique strengths to drive success in the business world. As an Empath Executive, you have the ability to connect with your employees on a deeper level, understand their emotions, and lead with authenticity and vulnerability. By harnessing your empathy, you can inspire and empower your team to reach new heights and drive innovation and creativity in the workplace.

Managing emotions in high-pressure situations is a key skill for any executive, but as an empath, it can be even more challenging. It is important to find healthy ways to cope with stress and not let your emotions overwhelm you. By practicing mindfulness, self-care, and seeking support when needed, you can navigate through tough situations with grace and composure.

Balancing empathy with assertiveness in leadership is a delicate dance that Empath Executives must master. It is important to be empathetic and understanding, but also firm and decisive when needed. Finding the right balance will help you earn the respect of your team while also driving results and achieving your business goals.

Navigating office politics as an empathetic executive can be tricky, as you may be more sensitive to power dynamics and interpersonal conflicts. It is important to stay true to your values, communicate openly and honestly, and build strong relationships with your colleagues. By staying true to yourself and leading with integrity, you can navigate office politics with grace and professionalism.

In the fast-paced world of business, it is easy for Empath Executives to experience burnout and compassion fatigue. It is important to prioritize self-care, set boundaries, and seek support when needed. By taking care of yourself and practicing emotional intelligence, you can drive business success while also maintaining your well-being and thriving in your role as an empathetic leader.

www.ingramcontent.com/pod-product-compliance
Lightning Source LLC
Chambersburg PA
CBHW030038230526
45472CB00002B/564